Tapping with Terri

IMPROVING THE CLASSROOM EXPERIENCE

EDUCATIONAL MANUAL
FOR TEACHERS & EDUCATORS

Advanced EFT Practitioner
TERRI MAYS

WWW.TAPPINGWITHTERRI.COM

For Teachers and Educators

2018

Terri Mays
Tapping with Terri
801 S. Fairmont Ave Ste. 7 | Lodi, CA 95240
Tel: 209-400-4104 | Fax: 209-333-1905
Website: www.tappingwithterri.com
E-mail: tappingwithterri@gmail.com

This program has been written, compiled and edited by

Terri Mays

Additional editing and production has been provided by:

Lydia Losongco
Original Artwork by Juliia Mays

Tapping with Terri

IMPROVING THE CLASSROOM EXPERIENCE

For Teachers and Educators

CONTENTS

Foreword

Have you ever rubbed your head when you had a headache? Or pushed hard between your eyebrows or rubbed your temples when you were stressed or worried? We touch, hold, pat and rub ourselves for comfort. We feel powerful emotions…some feel bad some feel good. We talk to ourselves…even though it is often negative. The Emotional Freedom Technique or EFT is a soothing technique that releases our feelings of stress, anxiety, pain and distressing thoughts. EFT, commonly called "Tapping" is a gentle form of soothing touch that works with the body's energy system. This electrical or energy system that runs through our body is carried through tiny pathways called meridians. The same meridians they use in acupressure or acupuncture.

The research is in now and EFT clearly demonstrates that our mind stuffs emotions down into our bodies and there they stay until given attention or acknowledged for the psychic wounds they are. Just think about the name, <u>Emotional Freedom Technique</u>. By using this process, you can literally free yourself from your limiting beliefs, hurts and fears that cause so much anxiety, pain, depression and stress. The results that thousands experience daily using this easy to learn technique is nothing short of phenomenal.

Terri Mays, along with many other EFT or "Tapping" practitioners are now bringing this amazingly effective technique into the classrooms and teaching students as young as five years old how to "Tap" to cope with a myriad of changes in their home and personal lives as well as the overwhelming tasks of learning huge amounts of information to score well on state competency tests in order to "move forward". There are other stresses as well, like; moving to a new school, making new acquaintances, new teachers, new grade levels and stresses at home that "overload" these young people making it more difficult to keep up with the rigorous demands of school systems that often put more attention on performance than on social interaction and becoming well-adjusted human beings in our ever-changing world.

Today's teachers are also under tremendous pressure to perform, and this takes its toll on even the most dedicated of educators, causing increased anxiety over how to help their young charges move forward.

What todays teachers need, so desperately, in my opinion, is a tool that can be easily implemented to make the "classroom experience" more fun and less stressful while improving the learning experience for the students and at the same time empowering them in their social and home experiences as well. Every teacher, if they have the right motivation to begin with, will embrace and want to learn how to teach this powerful new tool that has been proven, through Gold-standard research to be the most powerful and effective anxiety-reducing and intelligence-increasing way to help students today.

I highly endorse Terri's work and have seen the amazing transformational results first-hand in our clinic when Terri works with students who are barely passing and apathetic about school, often bordering on clinical depression become "A" and "B" students who are now fully engaged in school, their social lives and even having a strong positive influence in their families.

Terri is truly a teacher's teacher. I am so happy you have picked up this book and I'm even happier for all the many young people who will benefit, as a result of what you learn here… if you apply it. A whole new world is awaiting you, so dig-in and start learning how to teach your classrooms this incredibly empowering weapon against failure and mediocrity in education.

— Dr. Mitchell Mays

#1 International best-selling author in "mental health" for;
MIND GATE: Demolish Fear, Overcome Anxiety and Create the Life You Want

MEET TERRI MAYS

Author and Presenter

Terri Mays has been coaching and teaching Emotional Freedom Techniques (EFT) or "Tapping" since 2012. She combines her experience as an advanced EFT Practitioner, Jack Canfield Success Coach with nearly thirty years in the healthcare field developing a unique get results Tapping working with educators and youths.

This book has been written to provide teachers and an overview of this incredible self-regulating stress reduction and goal achieving technique, Emotional Freedom Techniques (EFT) commonly called Tapping with the possibility of bringing it into their classrooms with confidence.

Introduction

I wrote this educational Tapping manual with the intention that it will provide a great kick-start for providing Teachers with enough knowledge to introduce Emotional Freedom Techniques into their classrooms. I've included some Tapping history, research, personal lessons with Tapping, a how-to-tap guide and some basic Tapping scripts for students. Since I work with educators and students, you may find at times I am sharing directly to you the educator and at other times how I would explain Tapping to a student. I believe so strongly in the positive results using Tapping in the classrooms and in personal lives that if I can encourage you to use Tapping each day, I know you would become a fan like me. Like all learning, repetition and getting students to experience results is what allows Tapping to become the students "go-to modality" when feeling frustration, anxiety, sadness, lack of focus or just plain resistance to change.

EFT Tapping in School

Demands on teachers are continuously increasing with new standards and technology. Students are presented with more rigorous and difficult tasks at the same time as heightened, emotional and physical changes. Tapping gives students or teachers a tool they can use any time they feel stress, anxiety or any uncomfortable emotion.

Most of us as adults have a few memories of a time in school that we still can remember clear as day that we wish perhaps never had happened. I know that in my fourth-grade class Mr. Johnson had students stand up at our desks and read "out loud" our essays that we were supposed to write about on whatever reading assignment he would give us. It was brutal. Not only did we always have to write and then read it out we never knew who he was going to call on. It seemed so much easier to just turn it in. When it was my turn every part of my body felt sweaty, shaky, nervous, dry mouth and all. Of course, any student chatter that I heard only confirmed in my

mind how dumb I sounded. Now I am not saying this was wrong to read essays because I am sure it just warmed us up for next year's "Mrs. McKees class" when we had go to the front of the class to read assignments. As a result of that experience I defiantly would not volunteer for things that sounded like it may have been fun to do in high school because I just imagined I would be repeating those 4th and 5th grade anxieties.

I share this because, had I known about Tapping on those early essay days I could have Tapped about my fear and anxiety on my way to school and would not been so nervous. This is huge for me today because, I actually like speaking and would have done so much more of it had I not had that program or memory always telling me "I am not good enough". Since learning Tapping I use it regularly before I do any public speaking because it raises my confidence and joy.

Research now shows that our common stress responses that we feel in our body come from an almond-shaped part of the mid-brain called the Amygdala which works as our personal alarm system and it controls the "stress center" of the brain. Think of Its job like the fire alarm that warns you to run out of the house… Sometimes there are real fires but often there are false alarms, perhaps from electrical interference or some prank. Your Amygdala (stress response) to keep you safe will always send the same signal –alert- "you better get out of there". It literally cannot tell if it is a false alarm or the real thing. If you think about how it's about keeping you safe, it could be fatal if you did not respond as if it's a real fire. Your Amygdala is sending this alert every time we feel any threat to our safety. Even if we think something is maybe going to be negative, scary or any kind of worry, it sends the Fight, flight or freeze response to your body. That why you don't just think stress you feel stress; maybe butterflies in the stomach, heightened blood pressure, tight muscles, sweaty palms or shortened breath.

Here's where Tapping comes in to help. Research at Harvard Medical School has shown that stimulation of certain meridian "acupoints" decreases activity in the amygdala, hippocampus (part of the limbic system) and other parts of the brain that deal with fears.

In a study using fMRI technology it was shown that Tapping on your meridian points decreases arousal in the amygdala. Demonstrating the amygdala "red alert" being reduced when the acupoints were stimulated, sending a calming response to the body. The amygdala now recognizes that it's safe. Amazing! I will touch on more research later because it is so exciting that EFT Tapping has been proven to reduce our stress and anxiety by over a hundred studies now.

Students and teachers are in a daily heighten stress and anxiety in the classroom. I have been told that emotions of Anger, Frustrations, Boredom, Stressed, Tiredness or Worry is common to be felt most classroom days. Since Tapping these meridian points while saying what they are feeling helps reduce the negative emotions. This then allows both the students and teacher acknowledge how they actual feel and shift into how they want to feel, which is proud of their results and achievements. This is particularly valuable when applied to anxiety or worries for academic test. My experience working with students they want to feel good about themselves but they literally are afraid to trust themselves in believing it. Tapping lets them realize that is a false alarm and they are bright and deserve to achieve their goals.

Stress Makes Us Stupid

There is not a class I have taught that has not all agreed they have experienced a time when they studied really hard, perhaps all night, yet the next day when they took their test they forgot even simple answers, that they knew they knew! That's why I say stress makes us stupid. When we are stressed or *worrying* how we want to perform on our test this signals the amygdala that this could be danger, not the results wanted and sends

adrenaline and cortisol (the stress hormone) into the body. When cortisol is flooding the body, certain body functions are heightened from the "fight, flight, freeze" response. Maybe wishing to run (not show up that day) fight (act out angry) or freeze (go blank- play dead).

This sends a signal throughout the body, "test" are not safe. All the fears of not being good enough, fear of failing, fear of forgetting only get confirmed stronger on the next test and so on.

Many researchers now confirm that with a more positive state of mind, cortisol levels in the body will naturally lower. The challenge is that our human brain has a "negativity bias", some say as much as five negative to one positive. It would make sense our first thought is always processing how we will mess up or feel bad. In a double- blind study (the gold standard of scientific research) conducted by Dawson Church, Ph.D., who studied changes in cortisol levels (the stress hormone) with conventional talk therapy and EFT Tapping groups. The Talk therapy group showed a 14 percent drop in cortisol levels, whereas the Tapping group dropped even more significantly showing an average decrease of 24 percent. Some participants even experienced as much as 50 percent decrease in their cortisol levels! This is far beyond normal cortisol level reduction results from previous studies.

EFT and PMR research in 2009, applying EFT Tapping and Progressive Muscular Relaxations (PMR) with high school students that demonstrated having severe test anxiety, results were significantly effective in decreasing test anxiety scores. This particular study showed both groups scored higher on the school test examinations; the Tapping group scored significantly lower on the Emotionality and Worry subscale. There are other studies but that is not my intention in this book to list the many research papers substantiating the benefits of Tapping. When I tell the students that research shows that after Tapping you can perform as much as 20% better on their tests and other performances, they always get smiles on their faces and start telling me that they will Tap.

EFT Tapping has been researched in more than 10 countries, by more than 60 investigators, with results being published in more than 100 papers and esteemed medical journals.

Where Did Tapping Begin?

Roger Callahan, PhD. (a psychologist who studied applied kinesiology with Dr. George Goodheart Jr., the founder of applied kinesiology or AK) had been doing psychotherapy for more than thirty years prior to his "aha" moment in 1979 with his client Mary. He had been working with Mark for more than a year. She had such an overwhelming fear of water that she could not even bathe her children with it precipitating an anxiety attack. She had constant nightmares about water. Although he had tried every anxiety reduction technique at his disposal with her, Mary couldn't even walk by the swimming pool on his office grounds without suffering.

Then one day, while working with Callahan on this fear, she complained about a feeling in the pit of her stomach, whenever she thought about water. Interestingly, there is an acupuncture point located directly beneath the eye that is linked to the stomach meridian. Callahan asked her to tap on that point while having that thought and they continued to talk about her fears. His thinking was that it might lessen her stomach pain.

When she did, instead of merely feeling relief in her stomach, she told him excitedly she knew her fear of water was gone. Quickly, she got up and went outside and walked into the courtyard that led to the pool and fountain. She walked near the edge of the pool at first and said that she felt totally free of the panic she'd felt for so many years. She then splashed water on her face with absolutely no panic feelings whatsoever!

As strange as it seemed, the process of tapping under her eyes, while she was talking about her fear of water, she had eliminated her fear. Her associated nightmares and headaches also went away and never returned!

Needless to say after this experience with Mary, Callahan deepened his study of meridian endpoints, combining traditional psychotherapy with Tapping on different parts of the body. This was the beginning of what Callahan called Thought Field Therapy or TFT. This was an important turning point and ushered in a new era of "energy psychology".

Gary Craig was one of these pioneers of "energy psychology". He developed a simplified algorithm for tapping points known as Emotional Freedom Techniques (EFT) that most people know today called Tapping.

> *"The cause of all negative emotions is a disruption in the body's energy system." - Gary Craig, Founder of EFT*

Help for Educators

Teachers not only have the challenge to educate for appropriate academic advancement but know they must wear multiple hats to keep student engagement, behavioral and emotional peace. Daily stress that can manifest in the classroom has the potential to effect memory, concentration, and problem solving ability that can lead to decreased student engagement. Research shows the experiences of youths play an important role in shaping the growth of the brain and its nerve connections as an adult. What we focus our attention on and what we spend time doing directly stimulates the growth parts of the brain that carry our complex concepts. We literally learn how to think, how to feel, why we do what we do and most importantly how we might do things differently during this time of our development. Studies prove heightened stress and anxiety reduce memory and comprehension, which is exactly what we are trying to teach our students! Wouldn't it be nice to have a tool that we can use anytime we must address various types of negative emotions? Now you do with Tapping.

WHAT IS TAPPING?

Simply stated, Tapping is a highly effective and clinically proven self-help stress reduction technique. EFT or Tapping works on the body's energy system and end meridians points. These are some of the same spots on your body that are stimulated by acupuncturists. But with Tapping, we don't use any needles! You can stimulate these meridian energy points by tapping on them with your fingertips. I like to call these points, "special bundles of energy" that help you feel better. The human body, like everything in the universe is composed of energy. The fact that physical human beings are comprised of electrical energy is a long-documented fact and medical science makes extensive use of electroencephalographs (EEGs) to record the electrical activity of the brain.

Harvard Medical School discovered that Tapping on these meridian end points communicates with the parts of the brain called the amygdala and hippocampus. The amygdala acts like our very own personal alarm system! Whenever you feel fear or anxiety the amygdala (part of your limbic system) is triggered to flood your body with adrenaline and cortisol, (commonly known as the stress hormone). This sets off the freeze, fight, flight response in the body. This response is described as part of our primitive brain response as if running from the tiger to be safe. Today, we don't usually have tigers chasing us but we get that same physical response with anything that doesn't feel safe. And we can get this reaction from nearly anything that worries us, whether it be an illness, friendships, performance, news events, etc, The list is endless.

Because you are saying what you are emotionally feeling while physically Tapping on these specific points, it is called "Energy Psychology". There are about thirty methods of Energy Psychology. Tapping is the most widely used and is now estimated to be used by ten million people worldwide.

You probably already do some of the Emotional Freedom Technique Tapping points without even knowing it. Have you ever noticed that when you feel stressed or upset about something you might put your hand on your forehead? Or, if you try to remember an answer you might put your hand on your chin?   if something suddenly startles you, you may grab or put your hand on your chest? Those are things we intuitively do to feel calmer and in-control of your emotions. Those are some of the same Tapping points that we use in the basic algorithm taught by Gary Craig, who studied under Dr. Roger Callahan (the discoverer of original Thought Field Therapy) in the early 1990s. Gary Craig a Stanford-trained engineer and performance coach transformed tapping into the easily acquired, self-administered tool used today called Emotional Freedom Techniques, (EFT). Because EFT is done by literally tapping on specific points with your fingertips, it is called "Tapping" for short.

Introducing Tapping to Students

As Tapping is being introduced to students of all ages, research demonstrates Tapping can improve academic performance, decrease negative emotional states, improve self-esteem and resilience and better solve negative social interactions.

Research shows EFT or Tapping affects positively both sections of the brain that play a part in deciding if something is a threat; the stress center in the brain or the amygdala, and the memory center, the hippocampus.

Here is a story that demonstrates how students learn to apply Tapping in their everyday lives. There was a student (we'll call her "Julie") that had learned Tapping at school and had shared how it helped her at home. The story goes something like this; Julie was excited because she had just got invited to her friend Mila's house tomorrow for pizza and movie. This was important to Julie because she had been feeling a little insecure with their relationship since they hadn't gotten together in a long time. When she came home from school all she could think of was what they were going to

do tomorrow together. When her mother came home from work the usual evening occurred with mom checking in if Julie got her homework done. Of course, Julie had forgotten all about her homework and telling her mother about going over to Mila's tomorrow. Julie's mother let her know that she's not going anywhere unless she has her homework done. Words fly from Julie how "she's not fair" and "doesn't understand me" and cries off to her room and slamming the door. After a period of negative emotions while lying on the bed she put her hands on her forehead, which reminds her about doing Tapping to feel better. As she Taps and vents out her frustration, she starts to think how her mother really didn't say she couldn't go she just has to get her homework done. She even thinks how Mila probably has the same homework to do. Now Julie can focus and begins to get her homework done feeling excited to let her mother know and finishing the evening discussing with her mother her plans for meeting Mila after school.

Students Catch on Fast

Students find their favorite points they like to "Tap on" when Tapping at home, quickly feeling the shift to feeling a little calmer. I like to think it's because they do not have the compounded interest, on their issues yet, as we have.

Tapping gives students something they can take ownership of because they can use it at their discretion, whenever or wherever they feel the need, which makes them feel safe and more in control, and that feels good with so much uncertainty and change happening so quickly. A good example that I've been told after I taught students how to use Tapping to help them reduce their stress and improve their test scores is that students have used it for various sport games and scored best ever!

"After learning Tapping with Terri my daughter made almost all of her serves at her volleyball tournament. She shared the technique with her team and the team went on to win 3 out of 4 of their games. Up until this point they had not won any of their games. It was awesome to watch!"

— Kari Boss - Nevada

Some students have even told me they use Tapping for their music recital or speeches. I am so proud that they recognize that it helps their performance. Even eighth grade students have told me they "Tap off and on" even though they don't know if it helps but they do it anyway! You as educators know this is a big win, eighth graders don't do anything they don't have to, especially something like Tapping unless they believe it was helping them.

The great thing about Tapping is it's quick, safe and easy to learn with excellent success rates even for complete beginners. I believe Tapping in our schools is critical as it gives students a feeling of control with their emotions they are feeling in their body. Higher sense of personal control may prevent illness and loss of self-esteem. Students learn to overcome stressful barriers that get in the way of learning and a happier engaged life.

EFT Tapping has been researched in more than 10 countries with more than 60 published results. Scientific research confirms EFT Tapping lowers the major stress hormone, cortisol.

"Tapping in school gives students the resiliency and ability to control their stressful thoughts and emotions, that can get in the way of learning," says Dr. Peta Stapleton.

Check out the video published by Dr. Peta Stapleton explaining her recent research on my website: TappingWithTerri.com

EFT Tapping significantly increases positive emotions and self-esteem decreasing negative emotional states. I encourage you to be open to possibilities. It's Time for a New Normal.

"Tapping is proving to be a powerful, well-researched technique".
- Harvard Medical School.

<u>TAPPING FOR TEACHERS</u>

Teaching is a stressful profession, even under the best of circumstances. You must be "on" nearly all the time. You are assessed on measures (such as student test scores) over which you often have little or no control. And, all too often, you're working without the resources or support you need to do your job well. Today, more than ever, teachers have a wide range of students in their classrooms coming from many different backgrounds and many different learning capabilities. Teachers experience students acting out emotions like anger and anxiety from home and social issues to test-taking on a daily basis. And, all the while, you are hoping to influence your student's minds to learning new things. Teachers are working longer hours than ever before, experiencing high levels of chronic stress which leads to premature burnout. Many teachers are contemplating leaving the profession because they feel overworked and stressed within five years! Stressful working conditions within any profession can lead to significant health concerns, both emotionally and physically. Wouldn't it be nice to start your day feeling calmer and more hopeful for improved student engagement and motivation? By incorporating "Tapping" in the classroom with your students, as well as in your personal life, you can!

I want to help you create the classroom experience the way you envisioned it when you first started your career as a teacher.

Research shows that Tapping is very effective for reducing anxiety, stress and other emotional issues and, it works on both real and imagined stressors. There seems to be no limit to the kinds of issues that Tapping can be used for to benefit those who use it. Trust the process more than you trust the fear.

"Everything you want is on the other side of fear." - Jack Canfield

Tapping can reduce or remove:
- **Anxiety starting school or a new class**
- **Bullying**
- **Exam stress – fear of failure**
- **Fear of Losing and making friends**
- **Performance anxiety in sports, competitions, grading etc.**
- **Jealousy or Rivalry**
- **Perfectionism anxiety**
- **Fear of learning something new**
- **Self-Doubt**
- **Learning Difficulties – Math, Spelling, etc.**
- **Grief – Loss of someone significant, loss of a pet**
- **Physical Pain**
- **General Anxiety and Stress**

Tapping is something that is best incorporated into daily life. The reason for daily tapping is life events are constantly changing. Finishing one lesson plan to move on to the next, home family interaction changes day to day often making it hard to focus on the daily lessons at hand. Beginning your day with 10 minutes of Tapping can help reduce the stress we may be feeling and allows clarity creating a more positive energy flowing. Just like

you don't do your stretches only when your back hurts. You can also use Tapping to clear any personal stress going on before going to your classroom. With all the uncertainty, you are subjected to in the news, Tapping can help you enter the classroom a little more at ease and free of anxiety. The more you use it personally you will discover opportunities during the day to Tap with the students. I have been told by some teachers that they have had students ask to Tap. That's pretty neat!

EFT or Tapping is rooted in sound science, and new studies are being made public every day. There are over 100 clinical trial studies on EFT, 43% the Gold Standard (Randomized Controlled Studies) and 98% of all studies show positive results. You can introduce Tapping confidently to your personal life and your classrooms.

TAPPING TIPS

The good news is, Tapping can be learned by anyone, even as young as four years old. If you're not familiar with Tapping at first it might look weird because you're going to be tapping different places on your face and body with your fingers. You can use all four fingers, or just the first two (the index and middle fingers). Tap with your fingertips, not your fingernails. The great thing about Tapping is that you can't get it wrong.

Your energy is all around you so you can Tap on the right or left side of the body points. You can Tap with either hand or even both. You can Tap on all the points or some of the points, just stimulating some of the points works too!

You'll be surprised after Tapping how big-deal things just won't bother you so much, it's amazing. The key is to give your feelings a voice as you Tap solidly yet gently on the energy points explained below, using two or three fingers with either hand, or both hands. Just start with saying what you are probably thinking, "I am scared about… or I am angry about"…. Then you can say something positive, what would you like to feel. "I am a really great kid/teacher". This is why Tapping is called "Acupressure for the Emotions."

Depending on the age of your class, you may want to focus on simple words they can understand.   Examples: "Even though I sometimes mess up, I'm a great kid".   You can also Tap while saying positive affirmations for the kids. "It's easy for me to learn new stuff", "I do great in school at everything I try", "I'm a smart kid", "When I study, school gets easy for me", "I'm a great kid and a great friend", "I'm proud of myself", "I'm awesome and I can do Anything!" The ideas are endless.

> *"The primary cause of unhappiness is never the situation,
> but your thoughts about it."* **- Eckhart Tolle**

TAPPING POINTS

Use the same amount of pressure you would use if you were to tap your fingers on a table, knock, knock, knock … You want to make contact, but not cause discomfort. Tap roughly five to seven times on each point. While there are many more Tapping or energy points you can use, I will just describe the most commonly used points. If one point is uncomfortable to do (like the one under the arm), then just skip it. You can Tap on either the right side or left side it doesn't matter. The order is not crucial either and you can even do the points in reverse. This algorithm below is commonly taught by most EFT Tapping teachers. The good news is that Tapping is very forgiving. A great thing to remember is this, you can't do Tapping wrong. So, just do it!

The basic 9 Tapping Points:

1   **Karate Chop** – the outside edge of your hand, below your little finger.

2   **Inner Eyebrow** – on the end of either eyebrow, near the bridge of your nose.

3   **Side of Eye** – the outside of either eye, on the bone.

4   **Under the Eye** – about an inch below either eye, on the bone.

5   **Under the Nose** – above the lip

6   **Chin** – below your lower lip, where your chin starts.

7   **Collarbone** – the inside end of either collarbone, below your throat,

8   **Under Arm or Armpit** – about four inches down, on the side of your rib cage.

9   **Top of the Head** – in line with your ears on the top of your head.

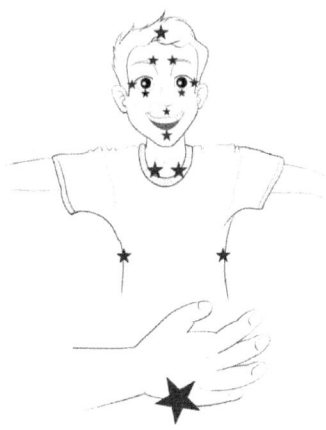

When you feel like you're done Tapping, take a deep belly-breath. (You do this by sticking out your tummy and breathe down deep like blowing up a balloon behind your navel then exhale). Belly-breathing activates the parasympathetic nervous system, which is your relaxing nervous system. I encourage you to add deep "belly breathing" to your classroom every day, the calming and focusing benefits are immediately noticeable.

Watch how to apply the Tapping Points at:
www.tappingwithterri.com/tapping

Just doing the Tapping by itself helps create a calmness. But to clear a specific emotional charge or feeling it's best to give yourself a voice. That's why it is more effective if you can say what you are feeling aloud while you Tap. This allows you to feel better and shift to more positive things you would like to feel. "If I didn't have this negative feeling, I would feel...."

"In our vulnerability we often mask our pain as anger."
- Jocelyn Kuhn

Special Message:
   ONLY TALK ABOUT NEGATIVE FEELINGS IF YOU ARE TAPPING, EVEN IF ONLY TAPPING ON JUST ONE POINT. The reason for this is that sometimes, just talking about the problem makes us worry more and it can get bigger. But if you Tap when you're thinking or telling yourself how bad you feel; it's resetting your energy meridian point to allow you to calm your body down about your issue or negative feeling, reducing adrenaline and cortisol allowing you to be in a more positive state of mind.

Many researchers have used electroencephalographs (EEGs) and taken EEG readings of electrical energy in the brain before and after Tapping. These studies show that when the subjects recalled events of stress while Tapping, the brain waves on their EEG readings were those that characterized relaxation or calmness.   Know that you can feel good about using EFT Tapping.

INTRODUCING A NEW PARADIGM WITH TAPPING

The more you use Tapping in your classroom, you will begin to recognize when a negative feeling is building up and will want to Tap on it together. Is there a test that the kids are acting stressed about? What kind of energy is gathering as the kids come into class? Taking five minutes to Tap to their feelings before that test or whatever they may be worried about can often switch frowns to smiles. Recently a Pacific Grove, California Sixth grade class introduced Tapping in the beginning of class every day and reported that students were more engaged and bullying was reduced, and their over-all performance improved.

See this interview at:
https://tappingwithterri.com/tappingforstressreliefinclassrooms/

THE TAPPING SETUP

I like to Tap on the Karate Chop point to set up my issue. You could just start Tapping but it's best to use a "Setup Statement" because it "sets up" the problem you are feeling. Otherwise, you may lose focus and our "busy monkey mind" may mess with you by jumping around from stress over the math test to stressing over chores at home. While tapping on the Karate Chop Point on your hand, you allow yourself to give a voice to your problem. In other words, you are listening to you. Your brain and body love it when they know you are paying attention.

It's good to start your set up sentence with "Even though I feel
_____mad,sad,etc_____, I love and accept myself" or any positive statement
you like. By saying "Even though I …" it allows you to be okay with what
you are feeling. Then follow up with saying a positive statement for the
second part of the sentence. I like to think of how I would like to feel such
as "I love and accept myself anyway", "I am a great kid", "I am a kind
person" or "I'm an awesome kid/teacher". You simply express the intention
of accepting yourself just the way you are. Say the words, even if you don't
believe them. You will find yourself shifting from unbelief to belief that you
are loved and acceptable, no matter how you feel.

<u>START TAPPING</u>

Don't worry if you don't get the exact point or what order you start for
Tapping, it's very forgiving even if you skip a point. I have a picture of the
basic energy on tapping points on the following page, so you can look at
them while learning to Tap.

This is the basic recipe of nine points that have been adapted from the
more complex algorithms by practitioners who found they can still get great
results and often even quicker. These are the points I use and students will
easily engage with great results.

Each time you move to a point, you can repeat the main issue you had
stated in the setup or, you can verbalize any feelings about the issue that
you are thinking; frustration, fear, embarrassment, etc. Don't worry if you
miss a point or mix them up. Remember, if you are Tapping, you can't get
it wrong. Just keep moving through the energy points. Each time you
move to a different point, just let your voice say what you're feeling and
continue tapping.

Sometimes, you may find when tapping on an issue you will start to feel lighter about it even after only a couple rounds of tapping on all the points. Other times, the issue kind of hangs on. Just keep tapping until you start to feel better. Tapping works so well, often clearing out negative feelings in only a couple of minutes. However, in this "instant world" we may think we're doing something wrong if it takes longer. The more specific about your issue the better. You might need to say or reword that "I still have some…" or "still feel somewhat upset about…math test tomorrow, etc   ". Remember you can't get it wrong, be easy with yourself, just play with it. As you start to feel better start to say more positive things about yourself and how you feel, such as "I Am Awesome!", then finish by taking…
A deep belly breath and blow it away.

If you just want to bring the kids together for something positive, you can just Tap while saying positive affirmations together. It's fun to get giggles and smiles. The reason you Tap while you say the affirmations is you are stimulating a part of the limbic system in your brain, which is part of the hippocampus, stimulating long term memory. Sometimes kids don't hear very many positive things about themselves, whether in school, on social media, or at home. Perhaps that's why so many students or young people retrieve into themselves.

Affirmations give us the fuel or momentum and positive reinforcement we need to pursue our goals. It may be unexplainable but what matters is that this technique does get results. It may sound like a far-out concept but it works.

"If you want to be happy, set a goal that commands your thoughts, liberates your energy and inspires your hopes." - Andrew Carnegie

TAPPING SETUP and POINTS

KC - Karate Chop Point

After saying Set Up,

Begin Tapping on Points

EB – Eye Brow

SE – Side of Eye

UE – Under the Eye

UN – Under the Nose

CH – Chin

CB – Collar Bone

TH – Top of Head

Take a Deep Breath….

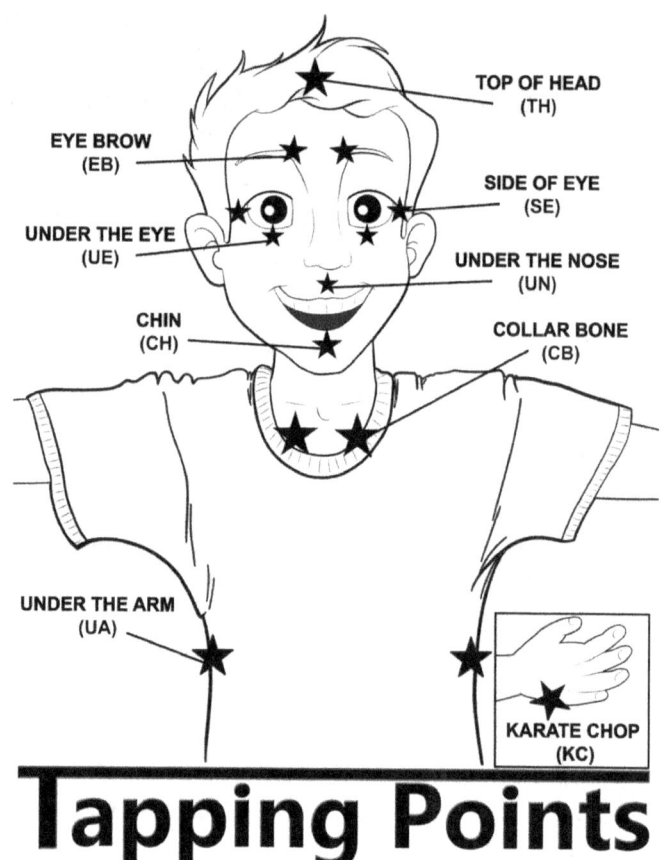

Tapping Points

One of the wonderful things about Tapping is this, you can Tap even when you go to bed. If you are lying in bed and you can't go to sleep because you are thinking about something that upsets you or makes you feel sad, then Tap. Let me share with you about a client of mine named "Matthew". He explained to me what was bothering him. Matthew goes to his Grandparents every day after school. He loves his Grandfather but sometimes they don't get along. This day he hadn't slept well because he was feeling upset at his Grandfather for calling him "lazy" for playing video games. So, we talked about how when he is lying in bed, he could Tap on being upset that his Grandfather called him lazy. As we Tapped on "being lazy playing video games", good times suddenly came to his mind about his Grandfather. He even saw what his Grandfather said really wasn't that bad and he laughed at how his Grandfather was wanting to spend time with him. We even joked about how he could teach his Grandfather a simple video, and how next time he was going to Tap whenever he was upset and feel good going to sleep.

Tapping can be used so many ways. What if a student has a big exam tomorrow but they heard their parents fighting. Now they worry about their parents; " they might get a divorce". Now, the student is feeling so stressed they can't study. They want to do well on their exam and make their parent proud yet find it hard to focus on their studies. They can Tap to calm their anxiousness they feel in their body, lower stress and allow them to not be afraid and choose to do well for their exam. The possibilities are endless.

SECRET TAPPING: STEALTH TAPPING

There may be times when you're feeling stressed, maybe you have a presentation or just nervous about something and think, "Tapping could help" but you would be embarrassed if people saw you tapping on your head so you don't want anyone to see you. Here's a couple of secret Tapping tips for you.

1. You can tap on your karate Chop point on your hand.
2. You can tap on your fingertips. Remember how we are Tapping on our bodies meridian points. You also have meridian points on your fingertips that parallel your face, head and body points. You can Tap or lightly squeeze at the base of the nail bed on the side of the thumb and fingers closest to you. Some are very clever and even Tap with one hand. These points are not as commonly used but are helpful when you are in a middle of a stressful situation and feel it's not appropriate to be tapping on your face or head. I like to think of the finger points as my "back up plan".

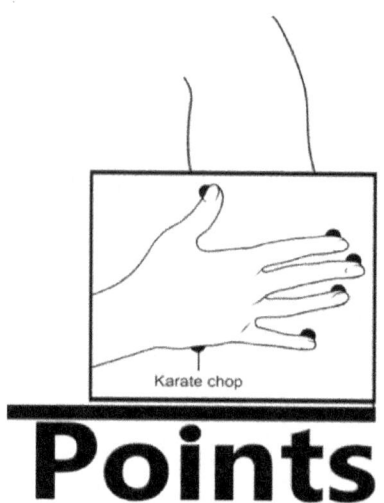

Karate chop

Points

HOW DO I KNOW WHAT TO SAY?

The real strength for effective Tapping is voicing words that connect to our negative emotions, limiting beliefs and the intensity of resistance we want to feel about something. I encourage you to feel the words with all the emotion and energy you can. Let your voice exaggerate your feelings, even sounding bigger than you might state them normally. Example; instead of saying "I am worried about my test". You could say.. "I am *really worried* about my math test". The following pages are sample Tapping scripts if you want help to get you started. If another word or feeling is more comfortable then substitute other words that relate more to your situation. Most often you will want to do the "Tapping round" several times. Most scripts begin with a negative round then shifting to a positive round toward the end as you begin to feel better. (This could take three or more rounds).

SAMPLE TAPPING SCRIPTS

The following pages are a few sample scripts and discussions that I have used with students that may be a help to you as you begin introducing Tapping. Also, there are many books with script ideas available. I list some of my favorites on my website, www.TappingWithTerri.com I am adding new videos and scripts to it regularly. I believe that it is always better to use our own feelings and words but sometimes scripts help us to get our words started. Soon you will just be Tapping in a free-form manner, easily Tapping to whatever feelings come up. Have fun.

AFRAID OF CHANGE

Anytime we are subjected to major changes, such as having to move to a new school, community or really anything new or unsure can send a signal of uncertain anxiety. Change usually is associated with stress. Triggering the Amygdala to release excess cortisol and create emotional unrest.

Think about what you are stressed about whatever change you are experiencing, then start to Tap on your Karate Chop Point on the side of your hand. Usually you start your Tapping at the Karate Chop Point saying aloud "Even though I"....; then finish your sentence with an positive affirmation. How would you feel if you didn't feel___?

Karate Chop: Even though I am afraid of having a new teacher, I'm still a great kid.

Karate Chop: Even though this change feels scary, I'm accept how I feel.

Karate Chop: Even though I am really afraid because I do not know this teacher, I know I'm a great kid.

Eyebrow: I am afraid my new teacher won't like me

Side of Eye: I like my old teacher better.

Under Eye: I don't know my new teacher.

Under Nose: I am afraid to change.

Chin: It doesn't feel good having so much change.

Collar Bone: I am afraid.

Under Arm: Part of me doesn't want to change.

Top of Head: Some of my friends like the new teacher.

Then take a big belly breath and blow it out. (like your blowing out your birthday candles)

If you are already noticing you feel a little less afraid, you can start to say that like; "I still feel a little afraid of…." It helps to be specific and say why you feel afraid.

Eye Brow: I still feel a little afraid of new changes including teachers.

Side of Eye: Change doesn't have to be scary.

Under Eye: I am a smart kid. My teachers always like me.

Under Nose: I might actually like the new teacher,

Chin: I choose to feel comfortable meeting my new teacher.

Collar Bone: I feel safe getting to know my new teacher.

Under Arm: I choose to be happy and feel good with my new teacher.

Top of Head: I'm an Awesome kid and feel good about myself!

Every time you Tap around the points or you feel like you feel a little different, Take a Deep Belly Breath and Blow it Away.

You will notice after a couple rounds it feels silly to keep saying I feel afraid of this "change", because it just starts to go away. Take a big breath and blow it away and SMILE. *You are* Awesome and better than you believe!

"If you don't like something change it.
If you can't change it, change your attitude." - *Maya Angelou*

When it comes to Test Anxiety, I tell all my students that Tapping may look silly, but research shows that students who Tapped, score up to 20% better on their tests. I'll take looking silly anytime for better grades, their eyes grow big and grin. I have gotten feedback from students they used Tapping for a test and felt they did better, time and time again.

Here's a simple script to Tap on "worries before an exam". Tapping could be used as a group exercise before any major or minor test the class may face. You can use any student's concerns or general statements such as "Even though I might have some stress about this test and I haven't studied enough for it, I accept myself anyway".

TEST EFT TAPPING SCRIPT

Setup:

KC - Even though I feel really nervous about writing this (_math_) test and my throat feels dry and I find it hard to swallow and it's hard to breathe. I am okay and I can try my best.

KC - Even though I'm worried that I won't do my best and show how smart I really am, I'm an great kid no matter what .

KC - Even though I am nervous it will be hard, I am a great student.

Continue Tapping Points.

EB – I'm feeling really stressed!

SE – I have to write a math test!

UE – My throat is really dry! It's hard to breathe!

UN – What if I don't know all the answers?

CH – What if I don't improve my score?

CB – What if I make mistakes? I will feel so dumb.

UA – Well, all I can do is try.

TH – Sometimes I feel so dumb during these test.

EB – All I can do is try my best.

SE – That's all I can do. Sometimes I'm proud of myself

UE – I'm scared I'll mess up

UN – I'll try my best.

CH – I really do know a lot!

CB – I am letting go of this fear.

UA – I remember what I have studied.

TH – I'm getting smarter every day!

EB – I actually like all the new stuff I am learning.

SE – I am a good student.

UE – Quitting is not an option.

UN – I'd rather be calm and confident

CH – I'm going to ace this test!

CB – I am a smart kid and I know what to do.

Smile… Take A Deep Breath and Blow It Away.

STUDENT TEST ANXIETY TAPPING SCRIPT

You can start with taking a deep breath in and blow it out. Then begin Tapping…

Karate chop: Even though I am *really nervous* about this test, I am a great kid anyway.

Karate chop: Even though I feel *really stressed* about this test and I almost feel sick in my stomach, I'm still an awesome kid.

Karate chop: Even though I am nervous about not doing my best on my test, I'm a great kid and everything is okay.

Eyebrow: I am so worried about this test.

Side of Eye: What if I mess up?

Under Eye: I'm so nervous about messing up.

Under Nose: So nervous I can feel it in my body.

Chin: This test is making me so nervous.

Collar Bone: What if I don't improve my score?

Under Arm: All I can do is try my best.

Top of Head: I am nervous how I will do on my test..

Eyebrow: I am so nervous I'm scared I will forget my answers.

Side of Eye: I choose to relax my body now.

Under Eye: I don't have to be so worried. I do know a lot.

Under Nose: I am worried I will mess up even though I'm smart.

Chin: I'm scared I'll make a mistake.. like nobody does that!

Collar Bone   I want to feel proud.

Under Arm: I can do good, my teacher says I am smart.

Top of Head: I choose to feel calm and chill.

Eyebrow: I know I can do well on this.

Side of Eye: I am feeling a little better, I will do my best.

Under Eye: I can let go of this anxiety now.

Under Nose: I know I will do my best, and my best is good enough.

Chin: I feel good learning new things.

Collar Bone: I am proud of myself and learning new things.

Under Arm: I'm an awesome kid, I can do this.

Top of Head: I am relaxing and feeling better, I know I can do well.

Take a Deep Belly Breath and Blow it Out.

After Test/Exams: Tapping can be used on any negative feelings _after_ a test/exam. "Even though I might not have done as well as I wanted in that test, and it was really hard. I am still a great student".

Remember, Just Tap to _anything_ you are feeling. If you are mad at yourself for not studying like you wanted Tap on that! Tapping is like magic for your stress hormone in your body. That is why all the research has showed that if you vent out your fears and frustrations while Tapping whether in bed the night before school or that morning of the test, you will get clarity and do better.

"FEAR OF PUBLIC SPEAKING" TAPPING SCRIPT

Take two deep belly breaths then begin Tapping

KC – "Even though I'm scared I'm going to mess up in front of the class, I'm a great kid"

KC - "Even though I'm scared to read my essay in front of the class, I'm a great kid"

KC - "Even though I'm scared I will be embarrassed speaking in front of the class, I am learning to be confident anyway".

EB – I'm scared of talking in front of the class.

SE – Standing in front of the class makes me nervous.

UE – I'm scared the kids will laugh at me.

UN – Having to talk in front of the class makes me feel sick.

CH – I hate having to speak in public.

CB – What if I mess up?

UA – I am scared I will sound stupid.

TH – What if I forget everything?

EB – I'm scared of talking in front of the class.

SE – I get butterflies in my stomach when I speak in public.

UE – I hate everyone looking at me.

UN – I have practiced and want to be proud of myself.

CH – I'm scared I won't remember what I have to say.

CB – Maybe it would be fine even if I did make a mistake? It's not like everybody's perfect.

UA – I am confident in other things. I can do this.

TH – Even if I make a mistake, I'm OK.

EB – I can do this talk, because I'm awesome.

SE – Maybe I'm not scared, maybe I feel excited.

UE – I choose to be calm and do my best.

UN – I do like speaking to my friends.

CH – I can feel brave and proud.

CB – I can just do my best, I like my subject.

UA – I am feeling a little better.

TH – I always do my best and my best is good enough.

Smile… Take A Deep Breath and Blow It Away.

Fear of "This Thing I Have To Do"

KC: Even though I'm holding on to this ___stress__, about this thing I have to do.. I accept myself anyway.

KC: Even though when I think about this thing I have to do, I feel like I'll never be as good as I want to be. I choose to accept and love myself anyway.

KC: Even though I feel all this _____in my body, when I think of this thing I have to do. I choose to relax and enjoy myself now.

EB: All this stress in my body.

SE: I'm not sure if I can do this. I'm not good enough.

UE: I can feel all this resistance.

UN: So many mixed emotions in my body.

CH: All this stress about this thing I have to do.

CB: This thing I have to do, Part of me doesn't want to do it.

UA: I feel really stressed and over-whelmed about this.

TH: I really feel afraid. No, I don't. Yes, I do!

EB: I don't know why I feel afraid. I've done so many things before well.

SE: I'm going to stop being so hard on myself. I am good.

UE: My body feels good when I have got done before.

UN: Part of me maybe doesn't feel I deserve to feel so good about this.

CH: I have gone through freakout mode before and I've done OK.

CB: I've been anxious and stressed for so long, I'm afraid to let it go.

UA: I forgive myself for being so hard on myself.

TH: This is a crazy new thing Tapping, but it does feel better.

EB: It's OK to believe I'm good at this thing I have to do.

SE: I've had many successes. I can trust myself.

UE: I am willing for this to be easy, without any fear.

UN: I choose to release all this stress and pressure.

CH: I see myself enjoying this thing I have to do and I am safe.

CB: I feel excited and relaxed. I feel good about this thing.

UA: I feel calmer in my body. I feel great. I am awesome.

TH: Wow, what a wonderful feeling accomplishing this thing.

Take a deep breath, as you exhale picture or hear how wonderful it is now that you have accomplished the thing you had to do.

<u>Too Hard... Script for Younger Students</u>

(Replace the subject with whatever is at issue, spelling, math, history...)

Take a big belly breath and blow it out.

KC: Even though I cannot learn my spelling words, I am a good student.

KC: Even though spelling is hard, I am smart.

KC: Even though I think I cannot do it, I am smart and I will do it.

EB – I cannot do it.

SE – I will never be able to do it.

UE – Spelling is hard for me.

UN – I'll never be able to do it.

CH – Spelling is too hard.

CB - I will never be good at spelling.

UA - I only like spelling some words.

TH - I feel proud when I spell my words correctly.

EB – I feel smart when I read and write new words.

SE - I am getting smarter all the time.

UE - I am good at everything I do.

UN - I can ask for help with my spelling.

CH - I am a smart kid and I do like spelling.

CB - I am no longer afraid of not being about to do it.

UA - I can do it. I have confidence.

TH - I think I can. I know I can. I will do it!

Take a big belly breath, like you are blowing out all the candles on your birthday cake.

Sometimes students are so worried about a problem they can't express words to Tap. This is when we just Tap together and I repeat what they told me "I feel nervous" as we Tap one round. You literally repeat together and say "I feel nervous".

Take a big belly breath,

KC: Even though I feel nervous I am a good kid.

KC: Even though I feel nervous I am safe.

KC: Even though I feel nervous I am a good kid.

EB: I feel nervous.

SE: I feel nervous.

UE: I feel nervous.

UN : I feel nervous.

CH: I feel nervous.

CB: I feel a little nervous.

UA: I feel a little nervous.

TH: I feel a little nervous.

Take a big belly breath.

Ask student if they still feel nervous as they did in the beginning. If they choose to say why nervous then just add their word they said.
Example: "I am nervous I will be late." Then you repeat exactly their words at each point then finish with big breath. Most of the time the student will feel lighter and come up an answer how they will not be nervous.

GOOD-BYE TO "Unhappy Thoughts" TAPPING SCRIPT

Now that you know how to Tap, here's some Tapping help for when you just feel unhappy, maybe you don't even know why your unhappy. Here's how you can Tap on that.

Somedays it just seems easy, to think unhappy thoughts. Everything is upsetting. Maybe you're thinking things like school is hard, worried about something in the news or people don't like me. The more you think about how bad you feel it feels like it gets bigger, soon your whole day is unhappy.

This is the best time to start Tapping! As soon as you notice unhappy thoughts bubbling up in your mind, take a breath and blow it out. Then I want you to start Tapping on your energy points and say all your unhappy thoughts that your thinking. Next, I want you to start saying Happy thoughts that you want to feel. Some of the happy thoughts might not be true yet, but go ahead and say them while you Tap to re-set your energy and create your day. Remember when you're Tapping it communicates with your brain to help you feel calm and confident in your body, so you will just start to feel better. The last part of Tapping is just saying what good things you want to feel. My favorite time to Tap is when I wake up in the morning. Sometimes I will Tap before I go to sleep if I had something that bothered me during the day, that way I can sleep better and wake up refreshed.

Remember, you can change the words that feel the best to you.

Karate Chop: Even though I think people don't like me. I'm great just the way I am!

Karate Chop: Even though I sometimes make mistakes, it's okay, everyone makes mistakes.

Karate Chop:	Even though I am afraid to speak up in class because my friends might tease me, that's their problem.
Eyebrow:	I don't like being afraid to just be me.
Side of Eye:	I worry if my friends like me.
Under Eye:	I'm afraid I'm not going to be good enough and look stupid.
Under Nose:	The kids are mean to me.
Chin:	Bad stuff always happens to me.
Collar Bone:	I can't do anything right.
Under Arm:	I am different than the other kids.
Top of Head:	They say mean or hurtful things and it makes me feel bad.

Take a Big Breath and Blow it All Out.

If the negative words start to not feel true now, start saying ideas you want to feel. This is where you create your day!

Eyebrow:	All my teachers and classmates like me and I like them.
Side of Eye:	I love to learn new things. Studying makes me smarter.
Under Eye:	Not everybody is the same as me, that's what makes us special and interesting.
Under Nose:	I believe in me. I am important.
Chin:	I am a good friend to myself and to others.
Collar Bone:	It's easy for me to make friends, I play well with other people.

Under Arm:	No one can make me feel bad about myself.
Top of Head:	If someone says something mean to me, that's their problem not mine. They don't have power over me.
Eye Brow:	Everyone deserves to be happy, that includes me.
Side of Eye:	I am happy. I am a smart kid.
Under Eye:	Life is fun, it makes me smile and laugh.
Under Nose:	I won't let anyone make me unhappy.
Chin:	I believe in me and I am important.
Collar Bone:	I care about myself and other people. I have lots of friends who love me.
Under Arm:	I was born to have a happy life and feel good.
Top of Head:	I am getting better every day in every way. I am an Awesome kid!

Take a Big Belly Breath and blow it out like your blowing out your birthday candles!

SMILE Because You just set your intention today to feel good no matter what!

Note: If a thought bubbles up of doubting yourself, you just Tap and tell your dumb fear: "*That's not true!* I am going to do my best and I am proud of me! In fact I am Awesome!"

Tapping communicates with that little part of your brain that sometimes is being afraid or negative. With Tapping you can knock it away. The good news is now that you know Tapping, you feel more in control of your body. In fact, you are the master and commander of your body; you can choose when you want to feel better about anything! Set up your intention for your day. Life is supposed to feel Good!

I DO NOT WANT TO DO HOMEWORK

KC: Even though I do not want to do my homework, I am a good student.

KC: Even though it's frustrating and I cannot concentrate, I am a smart person.

KC: Even though I don't have the energy to do my homework, I accept how I feel.

EB: I do not want to do my homework.

SE: It's too exhausting to do what I am supposed to do.

UE: I'm angry that I have so much homework.

UN: I cannot concentrate when I am feeling overwhelmed.

UM: If I do good on my homework it will be expected of me all the time.

CB: Studying puts me under a lot of pressure, I do not want to do all my homework.

UA: I wasted too much time to be able to do my homework today.

TH: It is my habit to wait until the last minute and habits are hard to break.

EB: I just don't want to use all my time doing homework.

SE: I cannot do it. I keep avoiding it.

UE: I know it is my responsibility.

UN: I feel frustrated doing my homework.

UM: I know I can get it done if I want to.

CB: I am capable of doing this. I can figure it out.

UA: I feel good when I do get my homework done.

TH: I like myself when I get my homework done and do it correctly.

EB: I can choose to do this homework, I am amazing.

SE: I am ready to complete this and choose to just do my best.

UE: I will do my best.

UN: Maybe it doesn't always have to be perfect.

UM: It feels good turning in my homework.

CB: I am a smart kid, when I focus I do really well.

UA: I am going to just get it done. That way I can get my homework reward.

TH: I am proud of myself accomplishing all that I do. I can do it.

After Test/Exams: Tapping can be used on any negative feelings after a test/exam. "Even though I might not have done as well as I wanted in that test, and it was really hard. I am still a great student".

OPPORTUNITIES FOR DAILY TAPPING

Dr. Peta Stapleton suggestions in her Tapping in the Classroom Program Tapping can be used daily in the classroom for the following:

> Before Test / Exams
> After Test/Exams
> For Public Speaking
> For Memory
> Specific new lesson or event
> End of Day

EFT STUDENT EVIDENCE RESEARCH

Here are just a few of the studies:

Boath, Stewart, & Carryer (2013) – Is Emotional Freedom Techniques (EFT) Generalizable? Comparing Effects in Sport Science Students Versus Complementary Therapy Students.

Following a 15 minute EFT workshop and 15 minute lecture on EFT, 46 students suffering from public speaking anxiety experienced a significant reduction in subjective units of distress and anxiety, however no effect on depression was observed.

Qualitative reports from students revealed the students believed EFT assisted in reducing anxiety by helping them stay calm and focused.

Sezgin, Ozcan, & Church (2009) – The effect of two psychophysiological techniques (Progressive Muscular Relaxation and Emotional Freedom Techniques) on test anxiety in high school students: A randomized blind controlled study.

- Of 312 high school students, 70 students who were identified as having a high level of   test-related anxiety were randomly assigned to a control group who received progressive   muscle relaxation techniques or an experimental group (EFT treatment).

- Both groups observed a significant decrease in student anxiety, however a significantly   greater decrease was observed for students who received EFT

- Both groups scored higher on test examinations following the treatment, however greater   performance was observed for the EFT group (though the difference was not statistically significant). **Jain & Rubino (2012)** – The effectiveness of Emotional Freedom Techniques (EFT) for optimal test performance: A randomized controlled trial.

• 150 undergraduate students from three different universities with debilitating test anxiety were randomly assigned to three treatment groups: – 1) EFT treatment (2 x 2 hour treatments), 2) diaphragmatic breathing (2 x 2 hour treatments, 3) or no-treatment control group. • Significant improvements in optimal test performance were seen for both diaphragmatic breathing and EFT on most assessment measures, with gains/improvements maintained at the end of the university semester when students were re-tested.

Fitch (2011) – The efficacy of primordial energy activation and transcendence (PEAT) for public speaking anxiety

- This study randomly assigned 82 university students experiencing communication/public   speaking anxiety into two groups: 1) primordial energy activation and transcendence (PEAT)   treatment (20 minutes in duration) or 2) no treatment control group.

- Overall, a significant reduction in anxiety was observed for individual who received the   PEAT treatment compared to the control group.

- Qualitative reports from participants also identified themes of effectiveness for the PEAT   intervention in reducing public speaking anxiety. **Jones, Thornton, & Andrews (2011)** – Efficacy of EFT in reducing public speaking anxiety: A randomized controlled trial.

- Significant reductions in public speaking anxiety were observed all subjective and behavioral measures following an EFT intervention.

- A significant reduction in public speaking anxiety (as measured by Subjective Units of Distress) was demonstrated within the first 15 minutes of EFT treatment, with further   significant reductions demonstrated at 30 and 45 minutes.

- EFT was found to be a quick and effective treatment for public speaking anxiety.

- **Fitch, Schmuldt, & Rudick (2011)** – Reducing state communication anxiety for public speakers: An energy psychology pilot study.

   Speech anxiety was significantly reduced for the 14 students (out of 67) who received   primordial energy activation and transcendence (PEAT).

   Qualitative reports revealed students who underwent PEAT reported an increased sense of   well-being and calmness, both during and after the process, stating it helped them maintain eye contact and was more helpful that other anxiety-reducing strategies.

Sporting/Athletic Performance

Church & Downs (2012) – Sports confidence and critical incident intensity after a brief application of Emotional Freedom Techniques: A pilot study. • Significant improvements in both emotional and physical components of sports

performance were seen after a single 20-minute EFT session, with all improvements maintained 60 days following treatment.

- **Llewellyn-Edwards & Llewellyn-Edwards (2012)** – The effect of EFT on soccer performance.

- • Results revealed a significant improvement in goal scoring ability from a dead ball situation   following a short EFT session. **Church (2009)** – The effect of EFT (Emotional Freedom Techniques) on athletic performance: A randomized controlled blind trial • FollowingasingleEFTtreatment(15minutes)asampleofcollegebasketbal lteammembers   improved on average 20.8% in free throws, compared to the control group (no treatment) who decreased on average 16.6% in free throw ability, thus suggesting EFT may improve free throw performance.

Learning Disabilities/Educational

- **McCallion (2012)** – Emotional freedom techniques for dyslexia: A case study • By the end of three EFT sessions, the client (who suffered from dyslexia) was able to read
- easily and fluently, and understand sentences. The disorientation associated with the client's dyslexia had also reduced significantly to a point where it was no longer an issue.

EFT Research/References

Baker, A. H., & Siegel, L. S. (2010). Emotional freedom techniques (EFT) reduce intense fears: A partial replication and extension of Wells et al. (2003). *Energy Psychology: Theory, Research, & Treatment, 2*, 13-30. doi:10.9769.EPJ.2010.2.2.AHB

Benor, D. J., Ledger, K., Toussaint, L., Hett, G., & Zaccaro, D. (2009). Pilot study of Emotional Freedom Technique (EFT), Wholistic Hybrid derived from EMDR and EFT (WHEE) and Cognitive Behavioral Therapy (CBT) for treatment of test anxiety in university students. *Explore, 5.*

Boath, E., Stewart, A., & Carryer, A. (2013). Tapping for success: A pilot study to explore if Emotional Freedom Techniques (EFT) can reduce anxiety and enhance academic performance in University students. *Innovative Practice in Higher Education, 1.*

Bougea, A., Spandideas, N., Alexopoulos, E., Thomaides, T., Chrousos, G. P., & Darviri, C. (2013). Effect of the Emotional Freedom Technique on perceived stress, quality of life, and cortisol salivary levels in tension-type headache sufferers: A randomized controlled trial. *Explore, 9,* 91–99. doi:10.1016/j.explore.2012.12.005

Reduces Cortisol

Dr. Dawson Church one of the world's leading experts in energy psychology discovered EFT Tapping reduces the major stress hormone, cortisol as far back as the 1980's. He conducted a double-blind study, the control group, which received conventional talk therapy, showed a 14 percent drop of cortisol levels, whereas the Tapping group showed an average of 24 percent decrease. Some of the Tapping participants experienced a decrease as much as 50 percent in their cortisol. With both groups, these changes were done within a one hour time period. This is huge! Since we know excess cortisol is what causes so much of our negative physical conditions like pain or an upset stomach. Sound familiar around exam time? We see this increased cortisol stress reaction even in the everyday work place.

As it is being introduced to students of all ages, research is constantly being revealed that it can improve their academic performance, decrease negative emotional states, improve self-esteem, improved sports performance and better solve negative social interactions.

"Tapping is proving to be a powerful, well-researched technique" - Harvard Medical School

To see the list of over a dozen research studies, go to <u>www.TappingWithTerri.com/research</u>

RECOMMENDED READING AND RESOURCES

- The Tapping Solution DVD
- The Tapping Solution; A Revolutionary System for Stress-Free Living by Nick Ortner
- Good Bye Ouchies and Grochies Hello Happy Feelings- EFT for Kids of All Ages by Lynne Namka, Ed.D.
- The Wizard's Wish by Brad Yates
- The Tapping Solution for Teenage Girls by Christine Wheeler
- The Tapping Solution; for Parents, Children & Teenagers by Nick Ortner
- The Genie in Your Genes by Dawson Church, PhD.
- Brainstorm the Power and Purpose of the Teenage Brain by Daniel J. Siegel, M.D.

PRECAUTIONS and DISCLAIMER USING EFT TAPPING THERAPY
Even though findings regarding the positive effects of EFT are exciting, researchers point out that EFT should not be considered "standard treatment" for people with severe mental disorders and should not take the place of approaches like cognitive behavioral therapy. Emotional Freedom Techniques (Tapping) should be thought of as an "adjunct therapy" and should be used in combination with things like a healthy lifestyle (eating a nutritious diet and getting enough exercise), traditional therapy, or other stress-relieving practices.

MORE ABOUT THE AUTHOR

Terri Mays is an Advanced EFT Tapping Practitioner, Certified Jack Canfield Methodology Success Trainer and Life Coach.

Terri loves teaching students and people EFT Tapping, how it allows you to master your fears and experience new freedom and possibilities. unlocking potential and maximizing performances with emphasis on self-esteem, personal growth and development. She loves helping to put the joy back into learning and the educational system _ with humor and inter-active learning by teaching Teachers and students how to Tap for everyday stresses and strains. She has been a healer and intuitive for over thirty years and is the founder and CEO of the **HOPEnUP FOUNDATION**, helping students in all areas of life challenges realize their full potential, self-acceptance and self-esteem with Tapping.

Her style is warm and fun as she includes her knowledge in EFT, NLP and Energy Medicine. She enjoys engaging students to experience their personal wins in whatever they feel may be holding them back. Sharing Tapping whenever she can and helping to empower their overall well-being and increased life energy is her mission of hope for our future generations.

Join our Tapping Community
https://www.facebook.com/tappingwithterri
https://www.instagram.com/tappingwithterri
https://twitter.com/tappingwterri

Learn More How Terri Mays Can Visit Your Classroom or School:
www.TappingWithTerri.com | email: tappingwithterri@gmail.com
Phone: 209-400-4104 | 801 S. Fairmont Avenue. Suite 7, Lodi, CA 95240